WORKBOOK

For

How to Know a Person

The Art of Seeing Others Deeply
and Being Deeply Seen

EDWARD PRINTS

This Workbook belongs to

Name:

_____

Date:

_____

DISCLAIMER

This unofficial workbook is not meant to replace the main book but to serve as a companion guide to it.

Let's get started!

3

How To Use This Workbook

We appreciate you selecting this workbook. We are honored to be a part of your amazing journey, and we admire your dedication to personal and Business improvement.

This workbook has been thoughtfully designed to go along with the main book, giving you an interactive, hands-on experience to improve your comprehension and application of its concepts.

We highly suggest reading the main book before diving into this workbook. We now want to walk you through the vast terrain of this workbook as you begin your adventure through it. We have divided the subjects of the main book into 12 main Chapters.

We hope that this workbook will be an invaluable tool for you as you embark on your journey, opening new avenues for inspiration and self-awareness. As you study this workbook, we wish you endless creativity, joy, and fulfillment.

PART 1
ANALYSIS

Chapter 1 and 2 Analysis

Chapter 1 explores The author, raised in a Jewish household, who experienced a sense of being distant and aloof, which became a part of who they were. They wrote in high school and were admitted to the University of Chicago at age eighteen, where they were taught by Saint Thomas Aquinas by atheist academics. The author described themselves as a reserved individual who felt uncomfortable when others sought to get close to them. This suppressed way of life was fueled by a fear of closeness, vulnerability, and social awkwardness.

The experience of absorbing the blows of adulthood, such as broken relationships and public failures, opened him to deeper, repressed elements of himself. Becoming a father was an emotional revolution, and his journey toward becoming a whole human being started with a little event: he was invited to speak on a panel discussing the importance of the arts in public life at the Public

Theater in New York. The author came to see that living a life apart from life meant being cut off from oneself over time.

Social skills are becoming more important in our day of slow dehumanization. The way we treat one another in our day-to-day interactions determines the quality of our lives and the state of society. The greatest gift one can give to both others and oneself is the ability to recognize and comprehend others. It is practical to learn how to recognize and comprehend others, as well as how to instill a sense of safety, respect, and value in others when making significant life decisions.

In a crowd, there are two types of people: diminishers and illuminators. Diminishers make others feel small and invisible, stereotype and dismiss others, and are so preoccupied with themselves that they fail to notice other people.

Illuminators are socially conscious and have received training in interpersonal communication. Married couples often read each other less well because they have locked in an early version of one another and are less aware of each other's innermost thoughts and feelings.

The goal of this book is to improve readers' ability to see people and give them a sense of being heard, seen, and understood. Through investigation, the author discovered that variants of this skill have been developed by remarkable people in numerous professions, including psychologists, actors, biographers, teachers, and talk show hosts.

The author's quest for deeper comprehension led him to realize that it is a way of life rather than merely a matter of learning procedures. By changing their attitude toward others, being present with them, and striking up longer conversations, readers can enjoy the greatest joys of human connection.

In Chapter 2, the author discusses the concept of "Diminisher tricks" and how they can hinder our ability to perceive others accurately. People often draw conclusions about entire groups or individuals based only on their outward appearance, leading to a lack of empathy and understanding. Key causes of this inability include self-centeredness, anxiety, lesser-mindedness, objectivism, and essentialism.

Objectivism offers an alternative perspective on human nature, but it can be challenging to see the most significant aspects of an individual, such as their imagination, feelings, desires, inventiveness, intuitions, faith, emotions, and attachments. The author has gained extensive knowledge from reading hundreds of publications written by scholarly academics who study human nature and have discussed their own unique lives with thousands of others. They believe that every individual life is more remarkable and unpredictable than any generalizations that academics or social scientists may make about populations.

Essentialism is the idea that some groups are fundamental and unchangeable, which can breed prejudice and a propensity to generalize about other people. Essentialists are ready to classify large groups of individuals using preconceptions, which can be destructive and wrong. Additionally, they think that members of one group are more alike than they are, and members of other groups are more unlike "us" than they are.

A stagnant mindset can also make it difficult to view someone else. We have only a surface-level understanding of each person, and depending solely on our untrained methods of interaction with people can lead to mutual blindness and social ignorance.

In Fierce Attachments by Vivian Gornick, the author shows how it is unsettling to be unaware of the person seated directly across from you. She talks about her mother, Bess, who had always taken

pride in being the only working-class lady in a loving marriage in her Bronx apartment building. Her mother's sadness was deep-rooted and primal, suffocating the air and turning her kids into props for her play.

Throughout her adult life, Vivian attempted to break free from her controlling, challenging, and captivating mother, but she was always pulled back. The two Gornick women, who were fiercely critical, angry, contemptuous, and close enemies, embarked on lengthy walks about New York City. Their history of hurting one another is a personal factor in their division.

In summary, essentialism is a false and damaging way of seeing people, and it is critical to identify and deal with the problems that lead to this perspective. By prioritizing comprehension and resolution of personal struggles, we can strive towards a society that is more kind and inclusive.

Bess and Vivian, two characters in Fierce Attachments, discuss the difficulties and misery facing both generations. While Vivian contends that Bess's generation led respectable lives, Bess laments the loss of order, peace, and dignity in her generation. As they get older and more cognizant of mortality, their bond becomes softer as they become older and more aware of mortality.

The author emphasizes the importance of seeing others in their entirety and becoming an Illuminator, a way of life, skill set, and craft. This ability is known by terms from other cultures, such as nunchi in Korean and herzensbildung in German, and helps us understand people's complete humanity and how they may impact our lives.

Key Points

1. The author describes their experience of being distant and aloof as a child, growing up in a restrained Jewish family, and discovering a love for writing. They eventually come to appreciate emotional expression and vulnerability as a result of things like becoming a father and taking part in a panel debate.

2. This chapter emphasizes the significance of social skills in fostering communities and deep connections, citing the decline of these abilities due to factors such as social media, marginalization of humanities, and societal changes.

3. The author discusses two personality types: Illuminators, who are highly understanding and curious, and Diminishers, who make others feel small. They suggest that married couples may become less accurate readers of each other when they identify more with their former partners.

4. The author emphasizes the importance of understanding and experiencing someone's consciousness through genuine beholding, describing a life-changing experience of truly understanding their partner.

5. Chapter 2 explores "Diminisher tricks" such as essentialism, naïve realism, worry, and selfishness, which hinder proper perception of others, highlighting that objectivism and a static attitude are barriers to understanding people.

1. Consider a time when you had genuine understanding and visibility from someone. How did the incident affect your relationship with that person, and what made it unique?

_____

_____

_____

_____

2. Think about your social abilities. Do you have confidence in any particular areas, and are there any areas you'd like to work on improving? In the era of social media, how do you handle social situations?

_____

_____

_____

_____

3. Consider a friendship, family member, or romantic partner in your life. Do you ever have the feeling that you are either an Illuminator or a Diminisher? How can you become more adept at comprehending and appreciating other people?

_____

_____

_____

_____

_____

Exercises

1. *Consider how social media affects your life. Does it help or hinder you when it comes to forming real connections?*

---

b. what are the adjustments you wish to make to the way you interact with people online?

a.

---

b.

---

c.

---

d.

---

2. What are your current strategies for dealing with vulnerability in your daily life?

Chapter 3 and 4 Analysis

In chapter 3, the author interviews LaRue Dorsey, a 93-year-old Black woman from Waco, Texas, who is known for her moral integrity and community-building efforts. The author explores the concept of attention and its influence on our appearance and social interactions. Dorsey initially appears strong and law-abiding, but when a white man named Jimmy Dorrell enters her diner, he smiles and hugs her, demonstrating his love and respect. This change in appearance changes Dorsey into a happy, content nine-year-old girl, a manifestation of Jimmy's attentiveness.

The author emphasizes the importance of understanding the influence of attention on our lives and how it affects how we connect with others. They argue that a person's gaze can highlight positive traits and determine their happiness. The author recommends treating others more like Jimmy, who extends a reverent greeting to each person and believes in their eternal soul with immeasurable worth and dignity.

Practicing Illuminationism involves offering a gaze that positively responds to questions about being a priority, being a person to someone, and caring about them. This approach exudes respect and acknowledges that each individual is unique and superior to oneself. The author concludes by emphasizing the value of treating individuals with warmth, deference, and admiration, rather than just observing or analyzing them. This approach promotes respect and belonging by better understanding and treating individuals as priceless souls.

The "Illuminator's gaze" concept emphasizes the importance of looking past egotism, anxiety, objectivism, and essentialism and focusing on traits like efficacy, compassion, responsiveness, active curiosity, and tenderness. Tenderness is the foundation of literature and seeing, and active curiosity is necessary for understanding others.

Affection views knowledge as an intellectual endeavor and separates reason from emotion. Human figures are judged according to how well they can mimic this loving mode of knowing. Leo Tolstoy argued that people are not like rivers, and every man carries the seeds of all human characteristics within him.

Most people will often fall short of the objective of being an Illuminator. By making an effort to illumine others with a kind, giving, and responsive gaze, we can look past the clichéd personas we frequently idly force on others.

Chapter 4, Oren Eiseley's "Flow of the River" explores the concept of the "extension of the senses" experienced by American naturalist Oren Eiseley while working in the Platte River field. Eiseley, who had a lifelong phobia of water, found himself ankle-deep in the river, realizing that it was part of a vast watershed running through North America. Despite his lifelong phobia of water, Eiseley turned over on his back in the water and floated, enjoying the experience and wondering what it was like to be a river.

In "The Flow of the River," Eiseley writes about

approach may be met with resistance from personal truths.

Individuals construct gates that can only be opened when it's convenient for them to do so and protect their psychological boundaries. To achieve life, one must approach it gently, much like one would approach a deer or a fawn nestled beneath a tree.

In summary, Oren Eiseley's "Flow of the River" emphasizes the importance of companionship, casual conversations, and patience in getting to know others. By being gentle and respectful, individuals can experience the delicate best of life, such as the touch, fostering stronger bonds and increased trust.

Playfulness is a key characteristic of accompaniment, allowing individuals to unwind, be authentic, and connect without even trying. Play is a state of mind rather than an activity, and it allows individuals to connect without even trying. When our minds connect and unexpected events occur, laughter arises, celebrating mutual comprehension and recognition. Gail Caldwell's autobiography, Let's Take the Long Way Home, shares her experience with a close friend who became close friends while participating in a play.

Becoming someone else's humble assistant as they create their music is a great way to support them on their path. The accompanist is not in charge of the trip but also not a spectator. It is important to respect another person's right to make decisions, as each person is on their journey and it is your responsibility to meet them where they are and assist them in choosing their path.

It is often a lovely thing to witness when someone gives up authority in exchange for companionship. Teachers have less influence over modern men than witnesses, and when they do listen to them, it's because they are witnesses. Assisting is an effective means of establishing rapport and creating a feeling of community, entails giving up control, enabling people to change, and developing trust. By doing this, we may foster a climate that is more welcoming and conducive to the success of others.

A good accompaniment is someone who knows the art of presence, which is being present at funerals and weddings, especially when someone is grieving or has been humiliated or set back. A heightened awareness of what they are going through at that precise moment can be this presence. David Whyte's book Consolations emphasizes witness, the right to be seen by someone and the equal right to be allowed to see the essence of another. Loren Eiseley's float down the Platte River illustrates a style of accompanying in the natural world, arguing that everything in nature is interconnected and that one can come to realize this by taking a seat back and allowing consciousness to wash over them.

Because of our shared humanity, everyone is related to everyone else in social situations as well.

Key Points

1. The chapter emphasizes the transformational power of attention on people and relationships, examining how attention can take on various forms, as demonstrated by Jimmy Dorrell, and alter appearance and mannerisms.

2. The Illuminator's View emphasizes the importance of loving, respecting, and adoring people, acknowledging their transcendent spark, and believing in the existence of a soul, to truly appreciate their existence.

3. The Illuminator's View embodies attributes such as affection, efficacy, generosity, receptivity, active curiosity, and tenderness, fostering profound understanding and admiration of others.

4. This chapter introduces the concept of accompaniment, an other-centered living method that involves patience, fun, and giving up control to build deeper connections and trust with others.

5. The chapter emphasizes the significance of being present for others during significant life events or challenging times, highlighting how showing up can effectively support and connect individuals.

Questions

1. Take into account the characteristics (tenderness, responsiveness, etc.) of the Illuminator's gaze. How can you use these traits in your relationships with other people to establish a deeper and more positive connection?

_____

_____

_____

_____

2. Consider a person who embodies accompaniment in your life. How do they manifest themselves to you in daily life or at important times? What characteristics make their presence noteworthy?

_____

_____

_____

_____

3. Take into account the idea of being present in your relationships. Have there been any instances where someone else benefited greatly from your presence? How can you intentionally show up for other people more often?

_____

_____

_____

_____

_____

Exercises

1. Take into account the characteristics (tenderness, responsiveness, etc.) of the Illuminator's gaze.

How can you use these traits in your relationships with other people to establish a deeper and more positive connection?

Traits	Area of Application
TENDERNESS	
RECEPTIVITY	
ACTIVE CURIOSITY	
ACTIVE CURIOSITY	
GENEROSITY	

2. who is the person who embodies accompaniment in your life?

_____

What characteristics make their presence noteworthy?

a. _____

b. _____

c. _____

d. _____

e. _____

3. Consider a momentous occasion in a loved one's life. How can you be more present and supportive during these times to foster a stronger bond?

Chapter 5, In December 2004, French writer Emmanuel Carrère realized that he had never truly loved his partner Hélène. They had discussed splitting up, but their distance was widening. The following morning, Carrère was in a depressed and disillusioned mood, having come to terms with the fact that he would eventually grow old and alone. They postponed their scuba diving instruction just before they left for home. When the tsunami struck the following morning, Carrère ran into Jérôme, Delphine, and Juliette, a French family. Carrère slid down a tree trunk to grab onto a palm tree after feeling carried away by a wall of whirling black water. He discovered he was still alive and had to save his wife when the water subsided. It was up to him to locate Juliette's body and return home to bury her.

Carrère's girlfriend Hélène provided the survivors with both emotional and practical support. She believed that helping the survivors was what brought Carrère and her together. However, Carrère remained inwardly focused, viewing himself as the dull spouse. After Juliette's passing, Carrère and Delphine visited a hospital to look for her body. They met Ruth, a Scottish woman who had been washed away by a wave together with her husband. Carrère and Delphine were aware of their responsibility to keep her from going into catatonia.

Carrère started to see Hélène differently after they got back to France. He wanted to live a lifetime with her because he felt sorry for her and decided he would live his entire life with her. Ultimately, they got married and had a daughter together, which is proof of the strength of human love and resiliency. Lives Other Than My Own, Carrère's book, is a moving examination of the mourning experience in humankind and the value of love and support during difficult times.

The Carrère vignette emphasizes the fundamental fact that each individual is a point of view, a complex picture of the world that incorporates memories, attitudes, convictions, beliefs, traumas, loves, fears, aspirations, and objectives into their unique perspective.

This perspective on the human being is known as "constructionism" by cognitive scientists. It acknowledges that humans actively create their reality rather than passively absorbing it. Making meaning of the environment requires the brain to use a limited amount of information, which is a radical process of building.

The human mind is also an amazing artist at creating a vibrant, lovely environment. People often slur words and pronounce them incorrectly, but their minds are adept at figuring out which words belong in which sentences, so they can infer a cohesive meaning from the words others say. Though our creative minds enable us to experience sound, music, tastes, aromas, color, beauty, amazement, and wonder, the universe is a dull, silent, and colorless realm.

The author highlights the effort our minds make to develop our identity, life story, belief system, and goals as she addresses the significance of creative artistry in our daily lives. Constructionism is recommended as a method of interpersonal interaction, which entails seeing people as active creators and gaining insight into their perspectives. To become Illuminators, we must comprehend the experiences and ideas that inform the answers we receive, pose questions, and actively engage with them. By taking this method, we can improve our understanding of one another and become more conscious of the models we employ to create reality.

Chapter 6 discusses the importance of having a conversation, which is an essential but challenging social interaction. A skilled conversationalist is someone who can delve into the inner workings of another person's mind and ask them how they view things. A good conversation is an act of mutual exploration rather than a succession of assertions directed at one another, provoking fresh ideas and changing someone's life.

The author emphasizes the importance of effective conversational skills and how it can be challenging for people to interact and comprehend others. They recommend viewing attention as an on/off switch rather than a distraction to improve as a conversationalist. The average person's speech rate is between 120 and 150 words per minute, which is insufficient to keep the other person's brain occupied. The SLANT method, which entails sitting up, leaning forward, asking questions, nodding your head, and listening with your eyes, is suggested as a way to improve listening skills.

Active listening extends an invitation to express, emphasizing the speaker's emotions and enabling more in-depth contemplation. Skilled conversationalists probe for details on certain incidents or encounters, going above and beyond to comprehend the other person's perspective on the matter. Looking back, it's critical to identify the lessons that were discovered and how those lessons affected them.

Don't be afraid to stop a conversation. While it might be enjoyable to finish each other's sentences or share amusing stories in some talks, there are occasions when thoughtful consideration is necessary.

An effective conversationalist manages her irritability and listens without interrupting to gain knowledge. Looping, which is simply repeating what the other person just stated, retains the other person's attention on their main points while making you listen more intently.

The midwife model is a communication strategy that is centered on supporting people in trying circumstances, such as going through a trying period or needing to make a significant life decision. A good conversationalist assumes the stance of a midwife, supporting a higher level of honesty and helping the other person become.

Maintaining the gem statement—the truth behind disagreements—at the center of challenging debates is crucial. It's critical to consider the fundamental reasons for the disagreement and the underlying principles to identify the disagreement beneath the disagreement. By doing so, you can prevent being a topping and foster a shared relationship.

As a journalist and Braver Angel, Mónica Guzmán emphasizes the value of being fully listened to in conversations and knowing what questions to ask.

Key Points

1. The devastating tsunami in Sri Lanka led to Emmanuel Carrère's transformation, causing him to reevaluate his relationships, particularly with Hélène, which ultimately led to their marriage and the birth of their daughter.

2. This Chapter introduces constructionism, which emphasizes how people actively create the reality they perceive, requiring the brain to work with limited information to construct a distinct perspective. Understanding this construction is crucial for appreciating various viewpoints and experiences.

3. Chapter 6 emphasizes the significance of meaningful talks, encouraging two-way discussions, and cooperative exploration. It provides advice on improving conversational abilities, including active listening and techniques like looping and SLANT, and emphasizes the importance of deep understanding and active listening.

4. The midwife model emphasizes the use of paraphrasing or repeating others' words as a communication technique, fostering deeper honesty and understanding. This approach, similar to the Quaker practice of a clearness committee, helps individuals navigate challenging situations.

5. This chapter emphasizes the importance of identifying common ground in disagreements, avoiding dismissive or competing approaches, building shared connections, and asking thoughtful inquiries to elicit the core principles of differences, thereby fostering a more harmonious and productive dialogue.

Questions

1. Think back to a difficult or transforming event in your life. What impact did it have on your outlook on relationships, morals, or personal objectives?

_____

_____

_____

_____

_____

2. Think about the notion of constructionism. In what ways do you deliberately shape the way you perceive the world? Are there any situations where your viewpoint greatly deviates from others'? Examine these variations.

_____

_____

_____

_____

Exercises

1. Evaluate your present ability to converse:

Have you used strategies in your conversations like SLANT, active listening, or looping? Give detailed examples.

STRATEGIES	EXAMPLES
SLANT	
ACTIVE LISTENING	

STRATEGIES	EXAMPLES
LOOPING	

Recall a discussion that significantly altered your perception of a person or circumstance. What aspects of it were significant, and how can you use those in your next interactions?

_____

_____

_____

_____

_____

_____

_____

Chapter 7 Analysis

David Bradley, a friend of The Right Questions, offers an analytical method for problem-solving by using index cards. He helps people stay focused on their objectives, abilities, and timetables by ranking their current activities on one card and their desired activities on another. This technique has been successful in his career due to his talent for identifying and selecting the right candidates.

David Bradley employs the "take me back" approach, which involves inquiring about an individual's personal life instead of their work life to ascertain their character. He focuses on high school experiences, highlighting their frailties and showing sympathy for the underprivileged and outcasts. With this method, he is better able to understand the generosity and fullness of a person.
\
Niobe Way, an instructor who taught eighth-grade boys interviewing techniques, believes that most

youngsters are excellent questioners, even though not everyone feels comfortable asking questions about themselves. In an interview, the author found that asking questions can be a risky move, as asking someone to admit they don't know anything can make them vulnerable. However, the essence of her work is questionable.

The author discusses the moral virtue of asking big, foolish questions in interpersonal relationships, arguing that thoughtful questioning promotes learning, humility, and respect for others. They also draw attention to the shortcomings of perspective-taking, which is unreliable, and perspective-receiving, which enables people to express their viewpoints and experiences. They caution against posing potentially detrimental queries that do not imply passing judgment or relinquishing control.

Open-ended, humble inquiries empower the other person to take the lead and steer the conversation in their direction. For example, a focus group moderator empowered a woman to express her joys and experiences in life by posing an open-ended inquiry regarding her recent trip to the grocery store.

An Illuminator can pose questions like "Where did you grow up?" and "What is the best way to grow old?" in social settings to find common ground. These questions can result in talks about cultural heritage, family history, and personal values. Common inquiries include "What would you do if you weren't afraid?", "What will we celebrate in a year?", "What chapter in your life is that you'll be celebrating?", and "Can you be yourself where you are and still fit in?"

The author emphasizes the importance of posing questions that inspire self-reflection and help people break free from ruts. They recommend posing questions about why people put off making decisions, forgive people they no longer trust, cause issues, and keep gifts hidden. They also discuss the difficulties gang members face due to past trauma.

In today's society, people often hesitate to have difficult conversations or ask personal inquiries because they worry about being private. Research indicates that people are often too shy to inquire, but deep talks about oneself are highly desired and self-presentation is a powerful human need. According to a 2012 study, disclosing personal information about themselves makes people happier than getting paid. Journalist Studs Terkel discovered that politely asking people about themselves encourages them to talk.

Key Points

1. David Bradley employs index cards to aid in problem-solving by focusing on objectives, competencies, and timetables, a methodical approach that has revolutionized task analysis and prioritization, making it a valuable tool for many.

2. Bradley uses the "take me back" approach to character evaluation, focusing on an individual's high school memories to understand their personal life and character, facilitating the disclosure of weaknesses, empathy, and understanding of the giving spirit.

3. This Chapter emphasizes the importance of asking thoughtful questions in both personal and professional life, as it fosters deeper connections, and promotes humility, learning, and respect for others.

4. Open-ended questions foster meaningful interactions by encouraging others to share their

viewpoints and experiences, making them more effective than closed ones.

5. This chapter emphasizes the importance of in-depth discussions in helping individuals break free from ruts and reconsider their life decisions. It encourages inquiry into decision-making, forgiveness, problem-solving, and appreciating the good things in life.

Questions

1. Examine how questioning functions in your interactions. Is it easy for you to ask questions? In your interactions, how does inquiry foster vulnerability and understanding?

_____

_____

_____

_____

_____

2. Think back to the recent discussions you've had. Were the inquiries closed-ended or open-ended? What effect did the questions' format have on the conversation's depth?

_____

_____

_____

_____

1. Make a list of your present objectives and pursuits.

a.
_____

b.
_____

c.
_____

d.
_____

c.
_____

How well do your objectives and current activities line up?

_____

_____

List three actions you need to take to align your activities with your objectives.

| 1 | |

2

3

PART 2
ANALYSIS

Chapter 8 and 9 Analysis

Chapter 8 explores how The Epidemic of Blindness and the Crisis of Connection has led to a significant loss in social ties, resulting in increased depression rates and suicide rates between 1999 and 2019. People now experience higher levels of anxiety, despair, and loneliness due to feeling invisible and socially isolated. Social detachment has destructive effects, leading to social isolation, mistrust, and a fear of close relationships. Individuals who experience loneliness and feelings of being invisible tend to become suspicious and take offense when none is meant, increasing their susceptibility to rejection and heightening their awareness and unease in social situations.

Loneliness obscures us, increasing our susceptibility to rejection and elevating our overall alertness and unease in social settings. Millions of copies of books about healing and healing from trauma have been sold, as have books about healing from trauma. People who experience sadness, loneliness, and a lack of acceptance grow resentful because they feel their identity is not acknowledged, leading to meanness and social isolation.

In 2021, hate crime complaints reached their highest points in a decade, and hate crime rates also reached their highest points in a decade. This crisis of mistrust is at the root of social breakdown, with societies with low levels of trust displaying impulsive sociability and disintegrating. Distrust breeds sentiments of vulnerability and exaggeration, leading to politics, which does not create a sense of community or connection but provides a sense of moral action and belonging.

Emotional and physical violence is a result of society's dehumanization and melancholy. Mass shooting perpetrators are often young guys experiencing an identity crisis, feeling like ghosts, and lacking in social skills. The propensity to eradicate another person's humanity is the core of evil. Factors contributing to this epidemic include social media, growing inequality, a decline in church attendance, a rise in populism and intolerance, the media and political elites' violent demagoguery, and a decline in community involvement.

The author contends that our social and relational problems are essentially moral, as we haven't taught people how to treat one another with love, generosity, and respect. Schools have traditionally focused on moral development, but after World War II, moral discourse and concepts have become less prevalent in American culture, demoralizing it. A culture where cruelty was accepted was created due to the disintegration of fundamental moral principles, leading to estrangement.

Chapter 9 explores the challenges faced by society in a time of extreme mistrust and resentment. The author shares personal experiences with victims of violence and discrimination, emphasizing the impact of media and cultural institutions on people's experiences. The author emphasizes the importance of understanding people as distinct individuals, members of groups, and participants in hierarchical structures, addressing historical legacies like sexism, elitism, racism, prejudice, economic and social dominance, and slavery.

Understanding someone well requires a combination of understanding them as a unique person, part of their group, and their social place. This requires graduate-level training in understanding others. Hard conversations often involve discussing differences and perceived power imbalances, starting with mistrust, hostility, and resentment. In 2022, a panel discussion about the "culture war" led to a difficult talk about the assault on African American history in schools. The author argues that the culture war was a larger conflict between conservative and progressive ideals.

The author reflects on the US's regressive approach to Black history, comparing it to the reactionary attacks on Black lives post-Civil War. The author felt helpless and terrified, and the panelists felt they should have investigated differences and respected each other's viewpoints. They learned from books and subject matter specialists that conditions should be prioritized in difficult conversations, as varying social dynamics and viewpoints can affect the outcome. The author also discusses Ralph Ellison's Invisible Man, which portrays the challenge of being invisible due to race. The authors of Crucial Conversations emphasize that communication occurs on two levels: official and real conversations. True discussion occurs through the flow of emotions, while official communication is represented by words. The volley of emotions determines the success of the conversation. The authors also remind us that every discourse has a framework, goals, and objectives.

The structure of a conversation is crucial for promoting polite and productive communication. Understanding someone else's viewpoint is essential for understanding their perspective and motivating them to elaborate. Curiosity is the ability to investigate something under pressure and under trying conditions. Respect and interest in the other person's point of view are demonstrated when one attempts to understand or step into their shoes.

In difficult talks, there is rarely a common knowledge base, leading to misunderstandings and negative motivations. To have a more fruitful and courteous discussion, assume the other person's point of view and push them to elaborate on their words. Negative motivations and misunderstandings can result from difficult talks, such as labeling one another, making them invisible, and stopping the discussion.

To redeem a difficult conversation, take a step back, analyze what went wrong, and separate, redefining the common goal of the talk and outlining one's motivations. This may involve broadening the objective to include both individuals. By doing so, you can create a more productive and respectful conversation.

Breakups can help build stronger relationships by allowing individuals to better understand each other's feelings and faults. Cognitive sciences show that people with varied life circumstances create different realities, with perception researcher Dennis Proffitt of the University of Virginia observing that people tend to overestimate the grade of steep hills. This effect can be observed in various contexts, such as baseball players, heavy backpackers, energy drinkers, depressing music listeners, and overweight individuals.

Difficult talks can result in misconceptions, but recognizing and resolving these problems can promote improved understanding and communication. James J. Gibson's thesis suggests that our affordances, including mental, physical, social, and economic capacities, shape our perception of the world.

Developing mutual respect and understanding one another's viewpoints is essential for developing empathy and mutual respect. Responding to emails with curiosity and respect can make the other person sound more humane and kind.

Everyone wants to be heard and for societal divisions to be healed, and every conversation starts with common pleasures, experiences, and problems.

Humanity is universal, even in challenging discussions. By honing our abilities and understanding others' perspectives, we can work towards a society that is more kind and inclusive, despite the challenges we face.

Key Points

1. The chapter discusses the rising suicide and depression rates, highlighting the link between social disintegration and a crisis of connectedness, exacerbated by loneliness, disapproval, and resentment in a cruel and remote society.

2. Over the past 20 years, the social breakdown has been largely caused by factors such as social media, increasing inequality, declining community involvement, and aggressive demagoguery from media and political elites.

3. The author argues that the contemporary social and relationship problems in America stem from a lack of moral formation and social skills, leading to a demoralized culture, acceptance of brutality, and alienation.

4. Resentment and feeling unrecognized fuel politics of recognition, leading to social upheaval. Loneliness and political activism are intertwined,

but relying on politics for personal issues may have negative consequences.

5. The chapter emphasizes the importance of having difficult conversations in a culture of mistrust and resentment, emphasizing the need to understand others as distinct individuals, group members, and participants in power structures.

Questions

1. Think back to a moment when you were alone or felt unappreciated. What effects did it have on your feelings and actions? Did it cause resentment or a need for approval?

_____

_____

_____

_____

2. Consider the idea of moral formation. How, in your opinion, are morality and social skills taught or not in modern culture, particularly in educational settings? How might societal problems be exacerbated by a lack of moral education?

_____

_____

_____

_____

Exercises

1. Make a list of the elements that you think are common in your community or society and that are contributing to the social breakdown.

a.
_____

b.
_____

c.
_____

d.
_____

b. Make a list of possible projects or solutions that could deal with the mentioned issues and aid in mending social ties. How can people and communities collaborate to create a setting that is more supportive and connected?

_____

_____

_____

_____

_____ 63

2. Consider how these elements have influenced your feelings, sense of belonging, and social interactions on a personal level. What are both the advantages and disadvantages?

ADVANTAGES	DISADVANTAGES
1.	
2.	
3.	
4.	

Chapter 10 and 11 Analysis

The author shares her experiences with bereavement, sadness, and supporting friends who are in need. Her oldest friend, Peter Marks, was a blend of ordinary and special, but in 2019, he started experiencing symptoms of sadness, leading to his death in April 2022. The author learned the value of making friends feel understood and supported during trying times and the challenge of education without magic bullets.

Peter went on to become a medical student, joined the Navy, and worked as an eye surgeon. However, the author soon discovered that he had additional childhood trauma, which distorted perceptions of time, space, and self over time. Depression is more than just sadness; it's a mental state that warps views of space, time, and identity. The author's eldest son got married two months after Pete's death, and the author remembers dancing at the celebration with his mother.

The author emphasizes the importance of empathy in human growth, as babies look for a caregiver to tend to their needs from the moment of birth. As we grow older, we internalize responses to fundamental life questions based on the people and things around us, sometimes unintentionally carried by parents and passed down through generations.

Stephen Cope, a psychotherapist, highlights the significance of empathy in a child's growth as it gives them a sense of security and worth. A person's quality of life can be greatly impacted by the quality of their connections, with the warmth of a family home being the most highly associated component during World War II. Men with positive ties with their fathers were happier in retirement, took more trips, and used comedy as a coping strategy, while men with strained connections with their mothers were more likely to experience prescription drug abuse, dementia in old life, and psychiatric hospital stays.

Will Storr's concept of a "sacred flaw" suggests that

people have barriers that affect their perception of the world. Overly aggressive defensive systems can lead to conflict and disasters, while introspection is overvalued due to the complexity of the mind. To fix one's models, communication is essential, and individuals need companions who can help them see themselves from the outside in and be empathetic.

Emotions are continuously experienced by our bodies, and the autonomic nervous system transmits data about these physiological states to the brain. Low emotional granularity individuals have a few emotional notions in their heads, while high empaths can discriminate between many emotional states with great detail. Different levels of empathy can be distinguished based on factors such as life experiences, genetic inheritance, and effort to develop empathy. For empathy and communication to be effective, a person must function at levels 0-7.

High empaths are highly perceptive and sensitive to all emotional cues from birth, and they are not truly alive until they are producing because of their overwhelming need to create. Empathy is a natural quality that can be acquired through facing and overcoming obstacles in life. Those who survive adversity but have not been broken by it emerge differently. Most sympathetic people have experienced adversity but have not been broken by it.

Developing greater empathy involves teaching the body to react transparently and communicatively rather than intellectually. People must go through experiences that are contrary to their past to heal from traumatic situations. Empathetic individuals can provide a physical presence by relaxing each other's viscera, co-modulating their heart rates, and creating a "higher vagal tone."

Emotions affect the perception of sight and sound, and fear changes how a person perceives their environment. Happiness increases peripheral vision and broadens focus, while anxiety decreases it. A person perceives the world as larger, more open, and happier when they feel safe due to the dependable and sympathetic presence of others.

Key Points

1. The author shares the tragic story of Peter Marks, her oldest friend, who tragically took his own life in April 2022 due to severe depression.

2. The "Art of Empathy" theory suggests that empathy's early development is a child's desire for approval and belonging from their caregivers, which can be influenced by hidden trauma that can cause emotional and spiritual harm.

3. Relationships significantly impact life quality, particularly during formative years. Good ties with parents, particularly fathers, improve mental health, while bad relationships can lead to dementia and psychiatric issues.

4. Will Storr's concept of a "sacred flaw" highlights how people's perceptions are influenced by their protection systems, and over active protection mechanisms can lead to personal and professional challenges, irrational behavior, and crises.

5. Empathy is crucial for effective communication and healing, developed through challenging times and life challenges. It involves letting go of guards and displaying vulnerability, enabling healing, and promoting healing.

Questions

1. Think about how empathetic you are. How do you react when someone else is in distress? Have you had any particular obstacles or circumstances in your life that have affected your ability to empathize?

_____

_____

_____

_____

_____

2. Examine how your early relationships—especially those with your parents or other primary caregivers —affect your well-being now. What perspectives have these connections given you on connection and empathy?

_____

_____

_____

_____

_____

3. Think back to situations in your life where healing —for yourself or someone else—was facilitated by empathy. How does empathy help foster a feeling of connection and understanding during trying times?

_____

_____

_____

_____

4. Think about the ways you can actively strive to develop greater empathy. What habits or experiences might enable you to let down your guard and accept vulnerability in social situations?

_____

_____

_____

_____

_____

Exercises

1. On a scale of 1 to 10, rate your sympathetic reactions in different scenarios (e.g., comforting a buddy, understanding a colleague's perspective).

1	2	3	4	5	6	7	8	9	10

2. Name three important connections you have from your youth or adolescence.

a. _____

b. _____

C. _____

3.Enumerate three practices or activities that you think could improve your empathy.

a.

b.

c.

Over the next month, make plans on how you will implement these into your daily routine.

Chapter 12 Analysis

These Chapters explore the concept of grief, trauma, and the importance of rethinking our foundations. Bob, the spouse of Barbara Lazear Ascher, received a pancreatic cancer diagnosis and was given a three-month prognosis. Barbara took Bob home from the hospital to make his last days with her more compassionate, but their grief was compounded by the feeling of a wind blowing through her hollowed-out body after Bob's death. She began to part with her possessions and subsequently came to regret it.

Greek is a process that frequently upends our fundamental beliefs about who we are and how life functions. Trauma puts our global meaning system to the test by presenting existential realities about life that run counter to it. Individuals who have experienced trauma and are irreversibly damaged attempt to incorporate the events into their preexisting models, while those who recover attempt to modify their models to fit the new information.

Rethinking and reforming oneself often entails embarking on the "night sea journey," venturing into the parts of oneself that have been broken off, rejected, unknown, unwanted, and banished. To truly understand someone, you have to understand who they were before they experienced their losses and how those losses altered their entire perspective.

Frederick Buechner and his brother were looking forward to taking their family to a football game in 1936. However, as their father peered in at them, they heard a scream and the creak of doors. They took several days to locate the suicide letter after learning that their father had killed himself by gas. Their grandma opposed their mother's decision to send them to Bermuda after a month or two, advising them to stay behind and confront reality. Later on, Buechner said that we should confront the enemy in all its dark might since reality can be terrible. They did, however, adore Bermuda, and they experienced some healing there.

For at least thirty years, Buechner's grief was

delayed, but it finally healed. When he noticed his brother weeping a year after their father's death, he knew that his sibling was grieving for him. His mother also shut down, even though she believed he had moved past the hurt a long time ago. Many years later, Buechner realized that the same steel that protects one's life from destruction also protects it from being opened up and transformed by the divine power that gives life itself its beginnings.

Teacher and author David Lodge explains that reading is 90% of writing, which is going back and editing what you've written. By presenting several viewpoints on a single incident and placing tragedy within the framework of a bigger narrative, the excavation job seeks to foster mental flexibility. Exercises that enable friends to travel back in time and rewrite their life stories can facilitate this excavating process.

The Illuminator ideal starts with a different conception of human nature and places a strong emphasis on the value of acknowledgment and social ties. Morality is a social practice that centers on treating people with kindness and consideration in particular situations. A person of character should assist others in healing from wounds and rebuilding their lives after losing a spouse or child. The Illuminator is a social, modest, compassionate, and caring individual who is there to recognize the depths of suffering and celebrate accomplishments.

Key Points

1. The chapter explores the profound changes individuals can experience due to loss, particularly in cases of disease and suicide, and how these events impact their overall meaning system and necessitate the incorporation of new conceptual frameworks.

2. The "night sea journey" metaphor involves reassessing one's history, particularly rejecting or discarded elements, and rethinking basic concepts like safety, deservingness, identity, purpose, and the nature of the world, as part of a reflective act.

3. Frederick Buechner's life story, marked by his father's suicide, delayed grieving, and eventual recovery, highlights the challenges of confronting difficult truths. Buechner's epiphany emphasizes the importance of sharing grief and vulnerability for transformation.

4. The chapter advocates for communal efforts in

delving into one's history and uncovering forgotten feelings, arguing that sharing personal stories can transcend fear, strengthen bonds, and foster understanding, ultimately promoting compassion and compassion through shared experiences.

5. The self-mastery and Illuminator ideal character development models focus on virtues like courage and honesty through introspective practice and individual willpower, while the Illuminator approach emphasizes interpersonal relationships, kindness, and thoughtfulness in specific situations, contrasting their respective approaches.

Questions

1. Consider a difficult moment in your life. What effect did it have on your overall meaning system, and have you integrated it or made accommodations for it in your current models? What basic concerns of identity, safety, and purpose emerged during this process?

_____

_____

_____

_____

_____

_____

_____

2. Examine your comprehension of character growth. Which model—the Illuminator ideal or the self-mastery model—resonates with you more? What impact do you think generosity and social relationships have on the development of your character?

Exercises

1. Narrate a memorable former experience that left a lasting impression on you.

b. Consider the feelings evoked by this experience. Were there any feelings you repressed or avoided?

2. Consider how you handle character development. Which model—the Illuminator ideal or the self-mastery model—resonates with you more? Why?

_____

_____

_____

_____

_____

_____

PART 3
ANALYSIS

Chapter 13 and 14 Analysis

In chapter 13, the author discusses the importance of understanding the personality traits of individuals like George W. Bush, who was known for his gregarious nature and ability to erase any distance between himself and others. Personality traits are dispositional markers that allow people to make meaningful contributions to society. However, the public discourse about personality is often misconstrued, with only 80 to 100 percent of respondents familiar with the Myers-Briggs personality testing and 0 to 20 percent familiar with the Big Five personality traits.

The Myers-Briggs test has been used to categorize people into thinking and emotional abilities, leading to false dichotomies. Empirical evidence suggests that individuals with strong cognitive abilities are also more likely to have strong affective faculties. The author concludes that comprehending the personality features of George

W. Bush is essential to comprehending the personalities of others, as a diverse range of human types is necessary for a functioning society.

Consciousness, conscientiousness, neuroticism, agreeableness, and extroversion are the Big Five personality qualities. Extroverts are kind, gregarious, thrill-seekers, and more chatty than silent. They are often fun-loving and more gregarious than retiring, fun-loving than sober, affectionate than restrained, and more impulsive than constrained.

Extroverts tend to be impulsive, risk-takers, and more prone to losing their lives in auto accidents. Low extraversion individuals tend to be more laid back, exhibit slower and less erratic emotional reactions and are often deliberate, purposeful, and creative. They prefer to be in closer ties with fewer individuals.

Conscientiousness is another quality that can help manage an organization, with high conscientiousness scores predicting positive outcomes such as longer life spans, better career performance, and higher academic grades. However, it is important to note that not all individuals with high conscientiousness scores have amazing jobs or live to be ninety years old.

In conclusion, understanding the Big Five qualities can help us better appreciate and respect the various personalities that exist in the world. By focusing on these characteristics, we can better understand and appreciate the diverse range of personalities that exist in the world.

Conscientiousness, neuroticism, agreeableness, and agreeableness are all qualities that can impact a person's life and relationships. High conscientious individuals excel in predictable situations but struggle in unpredictable ones, leading to workaholism, guilt, and obsessive behaviors. Neuroticism is characterized by a strong reaction to unpleasant feelings, such as dread, anxiety, humiliation, disgust, and melancholy. This trait can lead to poor relationships and less successful careers in youth and adulthood.

Agreeableness is another quality that can make relationships easier. People with high agreeableness tend to be kind, courteous, accommodating, and helpful, which can help them manage complex social relationships and be aware of others' thoughts. In choosing a spouse, it is advisable to prioritize agreeableness over neuroticism. However, any type of person can make a great spouse, and understanding these features is crucial for making better decisions.

Agreeableness is a mixed quality in the job, as those with high agreeableness levels may not always get promoted or make the most money. It is essential to understand a person's personality traits to handle them properly. Danielle Dick, a psychiatrist and geneticist, believes that there is only one parenting style that combines the unique personalities of the parent and child and that there is no perfect parenting style.

Personality psychology emphasizes being gifted and making the most of life. Charlotte and Emily Brontë's works, such as Wuthering Heights and

Jane Eyre, capture their distinct personalities. Personality traits, particularly neuroticism, can be developed throughout a lifetime, and as people age, they become more pleasant, responsible, and emotionally stable versions of themselves.

In conclusion, good parenting and cultivating harmonious relationships depend on an awareness of an individual's personality qualities. Living in a household with diverse worldviews can help individuals develop their identities and contribute significantly to their lives.

Chapter 14 explores Developmental psychology, a field of study by psychologists like Jean Piaget, Erik Erikson, Robert Kegan, Jane Loevinger, and Bernice Neugarten, which has been instrumental in understanding how individuals develop and change throughout their lives. Despite its outdated views, developmental psychology can help us understand others better by examining life as a series of routine duties. Life tasks are templates that identify typical patterns of human activity, helping us identify ways to resemble the template and ways to diverge from it.

The imperial task is a stage where people need to show others they are competent to develop a sense of agency. This can lead to suppressing weaknesses, focusing on interests, and using relationships as a tool. Interpersonal consciousness involves developing intimacy and a social identity through friendships and social standing. Successful people learn to be close friends, committed lovers, and intimate partners.

Interpersonal awareness allows people to have a deeper awareness of their values and experiences, while imperial consciousness can cause them to feel inferior and unconfident. Interpersonal consciousness occurs when people become aware of other people's experiences and the experiences of mankind as a whole, leading to idealistic impulses and a strong desire to form stronger bonds with groups. Breakups during this stage can be painful, as losing a spouse, friend, lover, or girlfriend can cause one to lose confidence in themselves and lose the internal organization that holds them together.

Career consolidation is another critical period of life, where people must discover their calling and contribute to society. Fit and experimentation are key to this, with an average of fifteen personal projects underway at any given time. Life can seem disorganized during this time, but eventually, many people develop a strong passion for a single line of work.

Individuals who consolidate their careers often adopt a more independent outlook and improve at managing their emotions and self-control. They may appear conceited and self-centered, but they will not reveal who they are until they reach a certain level of developmental selfishness. Intimacy motivation retreats during this stage, while achievement motivation advances.

However, most people rebel against this awareness when their sense of self is not satisfied by career achievement and they get weary of adhering to societal standards for success. For example, Le Suquet's owner, Sébastien Bras, realized that he had put too much pressure on his inventiveness to satisfy the Michelin system. The price of professional success eventually becomes too great, and the individual discovers they are spiritually unfulfilled and yearns to give selflessly to a cause and leave a legacy for future generations.

In the generative life job, people often find themselves no longer wanting the things they once did, leading to feelings of stagnation or inspiration. This can be seen in characters like Cristina Peri Rossi's short fiction "Breaking the Speed Record," where a runner who trains intensely to break a record finds stopping an overwhelming need. Adam Newman, a character in The Grant Study, was one of the saddest individuals due to his rigid family environment and loveless upbringing. He became a strict father at 45 and later became more self-aware and emotionally open.

People in this life task often seek ways to help the world, becoming parents and mentors. This shift from meritocratic logic to gift logic is a common aspect of life tasks. Leadership roles often lead to a creative mindset, which can divert individuals from their primary responsibilities. Wisdom is the ability to hold opposing truths concurrently in the mind without forcing them into a linear sequence and recognize the connections between things.

Life tasks serve as reminders that everyone is in a different stage of personal development, and a shift in circumstances often requires a complete overhaul of consciousness. Carl Jung suggests that we cannot spend our afternoons by our morning's plans, as what was wonderful in the morning will be tiny in the evening and what was true in the morning will turn into a lie in the evening.

Transitioning between tasks can be difficult, as progress is expensive and requires letting go of one's previous way of being in the world. To remind ourselves of personal progress and the value of accepting our distinct experiences and viewpoints, we can focus on daily activities. Self-discovery involves re-integrating into one's new attitude after removing one from it. Friendships are not unbreakable, but retirement, identity changes, and life crises all require a reimagining of reality, as they may not address issues at the same level of consciousness.

Key Points

1. The chapter emphasizes the importance of understanding personality traits as they significantly influence individuals' behavior and societal contributions.

2. The Myers-Briggs test is criticized for its misleading results and lack of scientific validity due to its reliance on false dichotomies, suggesting a shift to more reliable techniques like the Big Five personality traits.

3. The Big Five personality traits, including extrovertism, conscientiousness, neuroticism, agreeableness, and openness, are essential in understanding human personalities, each with its benefits and drawbacks.

4. This chapter introduces life tasks and developmental psychology, contrasting traditional stage-based methodologies and emphasizing the importance of identifying consistent behavioral patterns throughout one's life.

5. During the generative stage, individuals strive to assist the world and mentor future generations, shifting from a meritocratic career consolidation approach to an altruistic one.

Questions

1. Consider the qualities of your personality. How do they show up in your relationships, day-to-day activities, and decision-making? Are there any particular characteristics that you believe have had a major impact on who you are?

_____

_____

_____

_____

_____

_____

_____

2. Think back to your experiences taking personality tests such as the Myers-Briggs. Do you share the chapter's skepticism, or do you find them useful in understanding yourself? Which additional frameworks or techniques have you looked at for self-discovery?

_____

_____

_____

_____

_____

_____

3. Examine the Big Five personality traits: neuroticism, agreeableness, openness, conscientiousness, and extroversion. Which characteristics most relate to you? What effects do these characteristics have on the way you approach different elements of life and how you interact with others?

_____

_____

_____

_____

_____

_____

4. Consider the several life tasks (imperial task, interpersonal task, career consolidation, and generative life task) that are discussed in this chapter. Which assignments fit your life stage right now? Do you relate any particular difficulties or accomplishments with these tasks?

_____

_____

_____

_____

_____

_____

_____

1. **Enumerate the three personality qualities you feel most strongly represent you.**

a.

b.

c.

What are the benefits and drawbacks that come with these characteristics.

Benefits	Drawback

2. n a scale of 1 to 10, rate your level of agreement with the **Big Five** personality traits (extroversion, conscientiousness, neuroticism, agreeableness, and openness).

1	2	3	4	5	6	7	8	9

10

B. How do these qualities show themselves in your interactions with others, your conduct, and your decision-making?

_____

_____

_____

_____

_____

_____

Chapter 15 and 16 Analysis

Chapter 15 explores a recent interview with psychology professor Dan McAdams, the author discusses how people create their narratives and tell the tale of their lives. McAdams pays research subjects money for their time, invites them onto campus, and asks probing questions that elicit their personal experiences. Around half of the subjects cry at some point because they are remembering a difficult time in their life, while most tell him, beaming, that no one has ever questioned them about their life story before.

The author argues that people avoid discussing or asking each other about their personal histories due to rejection anxiety and social anxiety. Behavioral psychologist Nick Epley found that people underestimate the amount of information they will gain, the amount of conversation others want to have, and the speed at which others want to get intimate. People will gladly share their life tales if offered a little prodding.

outcomes such as longer life spans, better career performance, and higher academic grades. However, it is important to note that not all individuals with high conscientiousness scores have amazing jobs or live to be ninety years old.

In conclusion, understanding the Big Five qualities can help us better appreciate and respect the various personalities that exist in the world. By focusing on these characteristics, we can better understand and appreciate the diverse range of personalities that exist in the world.

Conscientiousness, neuroticism, agreeableness, and agreeableness are all qualities that can impact a person's life and relationships. High conscientious individuals excel in predictable situations but struggle in unpredictable ones, leading to workaholism, guilt, and obsessive behaviors. Neuroticism is characterized by a strong reaction to unpleasant feelings, such as dread, anxiety, humiliation, disgust, and melancholy. This trait can lead to poor relationships and less successful careers in youth and adulthood.

The author emphasizes the value of storytelling in conversations, emphasizing paradigmatic and narrative thinking. Stories show how a person's character develops over time and how little things can have a big impact on a person's life. The author contends that depersonalized cognitive patterns and misinterpretations of others result from our culture's paradigmatic richness and narrative poverty. They advocate for switching the conversation's focus to narrative mode to counter this.

Inquiring about people's objectives, values, childhood experiences, beliefs, and ambitions is essential. They also advise asking people about their upbringing, parents' objectives, and desires. For example, a woman who was let off her job discovered that her initial assumptions about retirement were incorrect and that she was not a good indicator of happiness. Her narrative left open-ended, and exuded preparation, acceptance, and joy for what lay ahead.

Creating an accurate and logical life story is crucial for living a meaningful life.

A person's narrative tone conveys their fundamental outlook on life and self-efficacy. The inner voice, one of nature's greatest marvels, brings seemingly unrelated occurrences together to form a coherent narrative with a clear meaning and purpose. It comes and goes, and speaking to oneself in the second or third person reduces anxiety, improves speech quality, expedites work completion, and improves communication.

Durham University professor Charles Fernyhough says that sometimes we hear our inner voice instead of speaking it. Our inner dialogue often consists of various mental personalities conversing with one another. It is crucial to pay attention to the voices and tones of the characters when hearing someone tell their story.

Identity is a complex concept that requires constant experimentation and a reliable identity. People often create their life narratives around adolescence or gradually over time, incorporating popular culture tales like "Overcoming the Monster," "Rags to Riches," or "Quest." Redeemal stories are often used to illustrate how people grow and mature due to negative situations, but it's crucial to assess the credibility of the narrator. Many stories are made up and flattering to themselves, while others may be deeply insecure and self-doubting.

Even evasive narratives, like the one told by Stephen Cope's mother, can be constructed from bits of truth but often omit difficult portions, leading to a lack of acceptance and understanding of one's identity and its challenges. Every chapter of a life story is preplanned and can be flawless or flawed, leading to narrative crises. Therapists can help individuals rewrite their lives and craft a more truthful narrative to help them navigate these crises.

Retrospective clarification, as defined by Philip Weinstein, is the result of selective ordering done after the fact. People's stories help us make sense of what we remember, recall what we forget, and familiarize things that once appeared foreign. By honestly and compassionately reinterpreting the past, we can make familiar what once looked foreign and grasp what we remember.

As we hear about people's lives, we become aware of our affirmations and acknowledgments, as well as the elements of the story that are successful and those that are not. Being open and honest about our flaws and strengths promotes growth and kindness.

Chapter 16 explores the story of Zora Neale Hurston, born in Alabama in 1891, who moved to Eatonville, Florida, an all-Black community. Her family was mixed-race and her mother was modest and driven. Growing up in Eatonville, Hurston learned the importance of individualism and community immersion. Her childhood memories are layered with emotion and memories, and she may never return to New York.

Artists who are now adults often go back to their childhood homes to find spiritual support and answers to why they are here. Hurston believed that every individual's awareness is shaped by the decisions made millennia ago by their ancestors. She focused on the experiences and viewpoints of distinctive individuals rather than clichéd characters or archetypes.

In today's identity politics environment, people are continuously limiting others to their categories, such as Black/White, Gay/Straight, Republican/Democrat, which dehumanizes others and fails to recognize individuals. To perceive someone fully, one must have two perspectives: one must see the influence of collective culture and the ways it develops over generations, and one must also see each individual as they go on a lifelong journey to create their own identity and worldview.

The idea that culture is either everything or nothing is among life's greatest myths. Every individual cocreates their culture; they accept certain aspects of it while rejecting others. Easterners are quicker to interpret someone's actions by examining the external environment and the circumstances surrounding the individual. We may better comprehend and value each person's distinct experiences and viewpoints when we recognize and value both of their qualities.

Our civilization is still shaped by the behavioral variations that existed long ago. Research shows that less than 50% of respondents from Japan and Singapore favored occupations where individual initiative was encouraged, compared to over 90% of respondents from the United States, the United Kingdom, the Netherlands, and Sweden.

Historian David Hackett Fischer emphasizes the long continuities that distinguish several streams of white Anglo-Saxon Protestant culture in the United States in his book Albion's Seed. About 350 years ago, groups of English people with diverse cultures and mindsets arrived in the same areas. New England had higher high school graduation rates and Massachusetts had lower murder rates.

New England and the Appalachian states have historically tended to vote similarly, with populist politicians doing well in both contests. For more than three centuries, this aggressive populist mindset has endured, and many of those who exhibit these actions are unaware of where they came from.

The author challenges readers to delve deeper into their selves and consider issues such as where they call home, how deceased loved ones manifest in their lives, and whether they accept or reject their culture. By talking about their heritage and the gifts bestowed upon them by their predecessors, we can start to see ourselves as full, embodying the spirit of history.

Key Points

1. The chapter emphasizes the significance of storytelling in promoting open dialogue, fostering understanding, and fostering a more inclusive society.

2. The author distinguishes between paradigmatic and narrative thinking, arguing that depersonalized thought patterns stem from our culture's tendency to be rich in paradigms and poor in narratives.

3. Understanding inner speech and identity formation is crucial for fostering genuine connections and shaping a person's storytelling style, as it reflects their unique personalities and worldview.

3. Zora Neale Hurston, an aspirational woman deeply connected to her cultural heritage, emphasized the individuality of each character in her narratives, opposing the categorization of humans.

4. The chapter delves into the impact of historical human behavior, settlement patterns, and cultural origins on attitudes towards individuality, gender roles, and social behavior in contemporary society.

Questions

1. Consider a particularly memorable discussion you had in which paradigmatic thinking gave way to narrative thinking. What impact did this have on your comprehension of the other person?

_____

_____

_____

_____

_____

_____

_____

2. Examine your internal dialogue. Which voices or personalities do you recognize in your thoughts? What effect does your inner dialogue have on the tone of your story and how you view the world?

_____

Exercises

1. Describe your inner speech's general tone. Is it encouraging, ironic, positive, or negative?

Consider how often you speak to yourself internally. Does it happen all the time, sometimes, or only in particular circumstances?

Describe your inner speech: is it coherent ideas, a torrent of thoughts, or something else entirely?

Chapter 17 Analysis

Chapter 17 explores that Wisdom is the ability to see deeply into someone's inner depths and how they should move in complex situations. It is not about knowing about physics or geography, but about knowing about people. Teachers, novelists, and history books all have their unique perspectives on wisdom, which can help them navigate life's pitfalls and navigate the dialectics of life.

The author's view of wisdom has evolved over the years, shifting from a conventional view of wisdom as a lofty sage offering life-altering advice. Instead, they believe wise people witness our stories and help us process our thoughts and emotions, navigating the dialectics of life. They are coaches rather than philosopher-kings, pushing us to clarify our true desires and explore the deeper problems beneath our surface problems. They create a safe space for us to navigate ambiguities and contradictions, creating an atmosphere of hospitality and honesty.

Understanding and wisdom come from surviving life's pitfalls, thriving in life, and having deep contact with others. The wise are those who have lived full, varied lives and reflected deeply on what they've been through. This perspective on wisdom is more effective than a generalized maxim or a simple lecture.

One example of this skill is writer Tracy Kidder, who met African man Deogratia in Burundi. Deo had spent his life in a rural village with cows, school, and family. After arriving in New York City with two hundred dollars, no English, and no friends or contacts, strangers helped him survive, and he worked as a delivery boy for a grocery store and slept in Central Park. A former nun named Sharon adopted Deo as her project, helping him find shelter, legal status, and a future.

Kidder decided to capture Deo's story in a book, Strength in What Remains, which created a rich, complex portrait of Deo and enabled readers to see the world through his eyes. Deo's brother was staying at Kidder's house, and Deo himself had gone back to Burundi to open a health center for the people he grew up with.

Lori Gottlieb, a therapist, shares a case study with John, a self-absorbed and narcissistic man who sought therapy for various reasons. Gottlieb initially treated John poorly, but she intuited that John had internal struggles and feelings he was hiding from, which she tried to address through compassion. She showed enormous forbearance, avoiding episodes when John was a jerk and waiting for a sign of bigger trauma. Successful friendship and therapy involve a balance of deference and defiance, showing positive regard while also challenging self-deceptions.

John's story about himself became less distorted as Gottlieb accompanied him, and he began to reveal experiences that he had been hiding. This story serves as an example of the gentle skills needed to be truly receptive, particularly the ability to be generous about human frailty, be patient, and let others emerge at their own pace.

Wisdom is a social skill that is practiced within relationships or systems of relationships, often formed when people come together to form a "community of truth." This community can be as simple as a classroom or as grand as a scientific enterprise and can be as intimate as one person alone reading a book. In a community of truth, people try each other's perspectives and take journeys into each other's minds, breaking free from the egotistical mindset and allowing us to take a journey with another person's eyes. The wise person is there not to be walked over but to stand up for the actual truth, calling the other person out when needed.

In a community of truth, people have a shared thought that is like a circuit in their brain. Cognitive scientist Douglas Hofstadter calls these circuits loops, and when we communicate and loops flow through different brains, we are thinking as one shared organism, anticipating each other, and finishing each other's sentences. This intermingling is not just about empathy, but the interpenetration of all minds in ceaseless conversation with each other.

In a book club, people can generate two sorts of knowledge: a deeper understanding of the books and a more subtle and important knowledge about the club, which is called "awareness," which is the highly attuned sense each person has for how the conversation should be pushed along. This awareness can only be achieved by a group of people practicing the skills explored in the book.

Magical moments in a community of truth occur when people deeply talk with crystalline honesty and respect. Kathryn Schulz's memoir Lost & Found highlights the importance of seeing and being seen in a community of truth. The author discusses their journey towards mastering the skill of seeing others deeply and being deeply seen, admitting that while they have made progress, there is still much work to be done. They aim to assess themselves honestly at the end of the book, focusing on two main issues: letting their ego take control in everyday life, possessing a natural diffidence, and forming easy intimacy with others.

The wisdom gained from this book has given them

a clear sense of moral purpose, aiming to cast "just and loving attention" that Iris Murdoch wrote about. Mastering these skills leads to acute perceptiveness, enveloping people in a loving gaze, and maintaining attentiveness even in the face of the world's callousness.

Key Points

1. The author's perspective on wisdom has evolved from a traditional sage-given advice to a practical approach, emphasizing witnessing and processing individual stories, guiding others through life's complexities, and acting as a coach rather than a distant philosopher.

2. Tracy Kidder's encounter with Deogratia and Lori Gottlieb's therapy case study with John emphasizes the significance of gentle skills in understanding and helping others, such as patience, compassion, and navigating human frailty, for personal growth.

3. Wisdom is a social skill that fosters a community of truth within relationships, involving genuine interest in exploring, trying different perspectives, and standing up for the truth when necessary.

4. In a community of truth, shared thoughts create mental circuits in multiple brains, allowing people

to think as one organism, leading to ceaseless conversations and interpenetration of minds.

5. The author shares their journey towards mastering the skill of seeing others deeply, acknowledging personal weaknesses, practicing vulnerability, and embracing compassionate awareness of human frailty.

Questions

1. Consider a challenging relationship or interaction you've had recently. How might applying the gentle skills of receptivity, such as patience and compassion, have changed the dynamics? How can you implement these skills moving forward?

_____

_____

_____

_____

_____

_____

_____

2. Reflect on a moment when you felt deeply seen or understood by someone else. What qualities or actions did that person possess that made the connection meaningful? How can you incorporate those qualities into your interactions with others?

_____

_____

_____

_____

_____

_____

3. Consider your journey towards mastering the skill of seeing others deeply and being deeply seen. Identify areas where you've made progress and areas where there is room for improvement. What steps can you take to enhance your ability to connect with others on a deeper level?

_____

_____

_____

_____

_____

_____

Exercises

1. Set two realistic goals for yourself in terms of improving your ability to connect with others on a deeper level. Outline actionable steps you can take to achieve these goals.

Goal 1:	

Goal 2:	

Actionable steps

a. _____

b. _____

c. _____

d. _____

e. _____

f. _____

g. _____

FREE AUDIO VERSION

As an Appreciation for Buying our Workbook and writing an Honest Review, we have decided to give you these Gifts!

Please scan the Qr Code Below.

FELLOW US..

fellow us on Amazon to get updated whenever we release our workbooks.

Scan the Qr code Below

Thank you very Much!

THANK YOU!

Dear Valued Reader,

We want to say thank you for purchasing our workbook, And we hope you enjoyed using our workbook.

Write a 5- Star Review!

Please, Leave a 5-star Review for this workbook. This will encourage us to keep Creating Quality workbooks in the future.

THANK YOU SO MUCH

PLEASE SCAN

Scan the Qr code Below to write a Review

Thank you very Much!

NOTE

NOTE

NOTE

NOTE

_____

_____

_____

_____

_____

_____

_____

_____

_____

_____

_____

_____

_____

_____

_____

_____

_____

Made in the USA
Las Vegas, NV
14 February 2024

85776388R00075